The Case of the Sneaky Stinger

W9-DEX-862

by Nancy Bentley

Illustrated by Hector Borlasca

SCHOLASTIC INC.

NEW YORK TORONTO LONDON AUCKLAND SYDNEY
MEXICO CITY NEW DELHI HONG KONG BUENOS AIRES

To Nick and Rachel,
the original Nature Investigators
—N.B.

To my wife, Silvana,
my daughter, Micaela,
and my mother, Perla
—H.B.

ISBN 0-439-47471-X

Text copyright © 2003 by Nancy Bentley.
Illustrations copyright © 2003 by Hector Borlasca.
All rights reserved. Published by Scholastic Inc.
SCHOLASTIC and associated logos are trademarks and/or
registered trademarks of Scholastic Inc.

12 11 10 9 8 7 6 5 4 3 2 1   3 4 5 6 7 8/0

Printed in the U.S.A.
First printing, January 2003

Book design by Jennifer Rinaldi Windau

CHAPTER 1

Nick and Kyle wrapped yellow and black tissue paper over their clubhouse door. Nick's birthday party was tomorrow.

Rachel, Bitsy, and Shelly sat on a blanket near the flower bed. They were having a tea party.

Suddenly, Nick heard his sister, Rachel, scream.

Nick and Kyle rushed over to her.

Rachel held her arm. She was crying. Bitsy and Shelly held their hands over their mouths.

"What happened?" Nick asked.

"Something stung me more than once," Rachel sniffled. A large red spot formed on her arm.

"What was it?" he asked.

"A bee," Shelly said. "I'm sure of it."

"A yellow jacket," Bitsy said. "I know bugs really well."

"A hornet," Rachel said. "It's my arm. I should know."

"Did it leave a stinger?" Nick took a magnifying glass from his vest pocket.

Everyone huddled around Rachel's arm. "I hit it really hard."

Nick leaned closer. "I can't see a stinger. What color was it?"

"Yellow," Rachel said.

"Black with yellow stripes," Bitsy said.

"Yellow with black stripes," Shelly said.

Nick took out his pencil. "How big was it?"

"This big," Shelly said, holding up two fingers an inch apart.

"No, this big," Bitsy said, putting her fingers closer together.

"No, it was THIS big!" Rachel said. And she spread her fingers far apart.

The girls started to argue. Nick shook his head.

"What were you doing when it stung you?" he asked.

"Having tea," they said together, pointing to Rachel's tea set.

"At least you can agree on something!" Nick paced back and forth on the grass.

"What's the matter, Nick?" Rachel asked, wiping away her tears.

Nick frowned. "We better figure out what happened before my birthday party."

He put his pencil into his vest pocket. "It's time for Nick Anderson, N.I., and Rachel Anderson, N.I., Nature Investigators, to go into action!"

CHAPTER 2

"Okay," Nick said. "Let's get the facts."
He pulled out his Nature Investigator
notebook. Everyone sat at the picnic table.

"First, tell me what you were doing," Nick asked.

"I already told you. Having tea," Rachel said.

Nick wrote down *tea*.

"Sweet raspberry tea," Bitsy added.

"Don't forget the cookies I made," Shelly said.

Nick wrote *cookies* in his notebook. "Then what?"

"We sat on the blanket near the garden," Shelly said.

"The next thing we knew, something flew all over us," Bitsy said.

"And before I could get away—POW! It stung me!" Rachel looked at her puffy arm.

Sat next to the flower bed, Nick wrote. He walked over to the flower bed. Butterflies, bees, ladybugs, and flies landed and took off from the flowers.

A hummingbird zipped overhead.

"Hey! Maybe it was a hummingbird!" Kyle said. Rachel gave him a dirty look.

"Hummingbirds don't sting people!" Bitsy said.

"Then what did?" Kyle asked.

"Yes," Nick said. "What did?"

"I don't know," Kyle said softly, his nose pressed against a flower. "But it sure is a jungle out here!"

CHAPTER 3

Kyle was right. It was a jungle out here.
Nick looked at all the bugs on the flowers.
Under SUSPECTS he wrote: *mosquitoes, flies,
bees, yellow jackets*, and *hornets*.

He scratched his head. There sure were a
lot of suspects. On the other side of the page,
he wrote the word CLUES.

"What did you see and hear before Rachel was stung?" Nick asked.

"A buzzing sound," Shelly said.

"Something flying fast." Rachel rubbed her arm.

"Something yellow and black," Bitsy said. "Just like those flowers."

Nick wrote, *buzzing sound*, *flying fast*, and *yellow and black* under CLUES. "Anything else?"

Rachel touched her head. "Maybe it wanted some tea!" she said.

"That's a silly idea," Kyle said. "Why would a bug want raspberry tea?"

"Because it tastes sweet," Bitsy said.

Kyle held up one finger. "I bet I know what it was!"

Everyone stared at Kyle.

"I bet," Kyle said, squinting his eyes and lowering his voice, "I bet it was a *killer bee*!"

The girls gasped. Nick dropped his pencil. Now they *had* to find out what it was! If they had killer bees in their backyard, they really had something to worry about!

CHAPTER 4

Nick was thankful when Kyle, Shelly, and Bitsy went home for lunch. His head was spinning. The list of suspects was so long he could hardly keep them straight.

"After the bug stung you, did you squash it?" Nick asked.

Rachel thought for a moment. "I sure hit it hard."

Nick jumped up excitedly. "Maybe it's still out there!"

After a half hour of looking, they gave up.

"I'll bring the blanket back into the house," Rachel said. Suddenly, she noticed a dead bug stuck to the edge of the blanket.

"It's the nasty bug that stung me!" Rachel said.

Nick brushed the dead insect onto his palm.

He took out his magnifying glass. "It's yellow and black and striped, but it's not fuzzy. I think it's time to go to the library." He placed the dead bug inside a small pocket in his fishing vest.

Later that afternoon, Nick spread his books on the back porch.

"Rachel, look at this." He pointed to photos of bees and wasps. "Bees and wasps are both yellow and black. They're alike but they're different."

Rachel looked at the pictures.

"Bees are hairy. Yellow jackets and hornets are smooth." Nick turned the page.

"Yellow jackets are wasps that build nests in small holes or in the ground. Hornets are wasps that make paper nests in trees. Bees build nests inside hives or trees."

Rachel studied the photos. Then she looked at the dead bug Nick had taken out of his vest pocket. "I still can't tell."

Nick nodded. What had stung his sister— a bee or a wasp? And if it was a wasp, was it a yellow jacket or a hornet? It was still a mystery.

"Maybe we'll know if we find the nest."

They walked around the backyard, looking for nests in trees, bushes, and holes.

Rachel found an anthill near their back fence, and Nick noticed a few cracks in the side of the house. But they didn't find a bee or wasp nest anywhere.

CHAPTER 5

Nick took the blanket from his sister. "Let's go back to the scene of the crime."

Rachel stood by the flower garden. Grass grew on one side. Dirt lay on the other. A short cement wall separated the two.

Nick spread the blanket on the ground.

"Shelly sat over there," Rachel said, pointing to one corner. "Bitsy sat here. And I sat right where you're standing."

Nick sat down.

"Then I put my feet on the wall near the flower bed," Rachel said.

"Like this?" He touched the cement wall. Rachel nodded.

Suddenly, a black-and-yellow insect flew up from the ground and started buzzing around them.

"Hey! That's exactly what happened before!" Rachel shouted.

Nick tried to wave off the wild buzzing thing, but it didn't go away.

"Can you tell if it's a bee, a yellow jacket, or a hornet?" Nick asked. He waved his arms in the air.

"See for yourself!" Rachel jumped back. "I'm not going to get stung again!"

Suddenly, the bug buzzed straight toward Nick.

"It's after me!"

Nick and Rachel ran for the back porch and slammed the screen door shut.

"It looks like the bug on the blanket," Nick said. "But what did I do to make it so mad?" Nick's eyes became wide.

"Rachel, I think we have all the evidence we need right in front of us!"

CHAPTER 6

"Let's go through our lists of clues and suspects one by one," Nick said. He opened his notebook. "What about mosquitoes?"

"A mosquito isn't black and yellow," Rachel said. "And after it bites, you itch. But bees like flowers. And we *were* sitting next to lots of flowers."

Nick smiled. "But bees are fuzzy, and the insect we found wasn't fuzzy. Also, you said it stung you more than once.

"A bee only stings once, then it dies," he said. "But a wasp can keep stinging and not die."

"The bug we found was dead," she reminded him.

"It probably died when you hit it," Nick said.

"Could it be a killer bee?" Rachel looked worried.

"Killer bees don't live around here," said Nick.

"Then, if it wasn't a bee, it must be a wasp. But what kind?"

"Hornets are bigger than yellow jackets. And they usually build paper nests." Nick held up his pencil. "We didn't find any paper nests."

"We didn't find ANY nests." Rachel put her hands over her eyes.

Nick walked to the edge of the garden. "Maybe we did. Look at the wall near the flower bed."

A small yellow-and-black insect flew by. Suddenly, it disappeared.

"Hey! Where did it go?" Rachel asked, leaning down.

"We forgot to look for nests in the ground," Nick said.

Soon, a yellow-and-black insect popped out of the ground near the wall and flew off.

"Oh, it was mad because I put my foot on top of its nest!" Rachel shouted.

"Let's look at the facts. It's yellow and black. Not fuzzy. It stung you more than once. And it lives in the ground."

"BUZZZZ! That means it must be a—" said Rachel.

"—yellow jacket!" Nick shut his notebook.

Just then he felt a sharp nip on his ankle. "Hey! A mosquito just bit me!"

Rachel giggled.

"Kyle was right," Nick said. "It *is* a jungle out here. Another Nature Investigator CASE CLOSED!"

BEE AND WASP FACTS

How are they alike?

- Live in groups and have a queen
- Help people by pollinating plants and eating pest insects
- Have yellow and black bands around their bodies, and two pairs of wings

How are they different?

BEES & HONEYBEES

- Round, hairy bodies
- Eat nectar and pollen
- Sting once, then die
- Live in hives

WASPS & YELLOW JACKETS

- Slender, smooth bodies
- Eat insects and sweet foods
- Sting many times but do not die
- Live in paper nests in trees or build nests underground

KILLER BEES

- Get mad easily
- Attack in swarms
- Live in the South and Southwest because they don't like cold weather

Run away if you think you're being attacked!

If you are stung by a bee or wasp:

- Carefully flick out the stinger.
- Put hot and cold compresses on the place that was stung.
- If you are allergic to stings, go to a doctor right away.